FORTUNATE EXILE

BOOKS BY IRVING LAYTON

Here and Now 1945
Now Is the Place 1948
The Black Huntsmen 1951
Cerberus (with Louis Dudek & Raymond Souster) 1952
Love the Conqueror Worm 1953
In the Midst of My Fever 1954
The Long Pea-Shooter 1954
The Blue Propeller 1955
The Cold Green Element 1955
Music on a Kazoo 1956
The Bull Calf and Other Poems 1956
The Improved Binoculars 1956
A Laughter in the Mind 1958
A Red Carpet for the Sun 1959
The Swinging Flesh (Poems and Stories) 1961
Balls for a One-Armed Juggler 1963
The Laughing Rooster 1964
Collected Poems 1965
Periods of the Moon 1967
The Shattered Plinths 1968
Selected Poems 1969
The Whole Bloody Bird 1969
Nail Polish 1971
The Collected Poems of Irving Layton 1971
Engagements: The Prose of Irving Layton 1972
Lovers and Lesser Men 1973
Seventy-Five Greek Poems 1974
The Pole-Vaulter 1974
The Darkening Fire 1975
The Unwavering Eye 1975
For My Brother Jesus 1976
Taking Sides (Prose) 1977
The Covenant 1977
The Poems of Irving Layton 1977
The Uncollected Poems of Irving Layton 1977
The Tightrope Dancer 1978
Droppings from Heaven 1979
An Unlikely Affair (Letters) 1980
For My Neighbours in Hell 1980
The Love Poems of Irving Layton 1980
Europe and Other Bad News 1981
A Wild Peculiar Joy 1982
The Gucci Bag 1983
Waiting for the Messiah (Prose) 1985
Dance with Desire 1986
Final Reckoning 1987

EDITOR

Canadian Poems 1850–1952 (with Louis Dudek) 1952
Love Where the Nights Are Long (illus. Harold Town) 1962

FORTUNATE EXILE

IRVING LAYTON

Canadian Cataloguing in Publication Data
Layton, Irving, 1912–
    Fortunate exile

Poems.
ISBN 0–7710–4947–1

1. Jews – Poetry. I. Title.

PS8523.A98F67   1987   C811'.54   C87–094320–0
PR9199.3.L39F67 1987

The publisher makes grateful acknowledgment to the Canada Council and
the Ontario Arts Council for their financial assistance.

Printed and bound in Canada
Book design by Linda Gustafson
Set in Weiss by The Typeworks, Vancouver

McClelland and Stewart
The Canadian Publishers
481 University Avenue
Toronto, Ontario M5G 2E9

*All of these poems have been published previously; a few have been revised
somewhat for this book. This selection was made by Irving Layton and
Russell Brown.*

This book is dedicated to Father Abraham and his amazing progeny

CONTENTS

Proclaim from every tower and from every steeple
He is our chosen God and we who chose, His people.

"Being elsewhere, the great vice of
this race, the great secret virtue,
the great vocation of this people."
— Charles Péguy

O JERUSALEM

Jerusalem, you will be betrayed again and again:
not by the brave young men who die for you
with military cries on their blue lips
— never by these
                        and never by the scholars
who know each sunken goat-track
that winds somehow into your legend, your great name
and not by those dreamers
                        who looking for the beginnings
of your strange wizardry ascend from storied darkness
holding dust and warped harps in their blistered hands

These will always find you and bring you
offerings of blood and bone
                        lowering their grave eyes
as to an idol made neither of wood nor stone
nor brick nor any metal
                        yet clearly visible
as though sitting on a jewelled throne
                                    O Jerusalem
you are too pure and break men's hearts
you are a dream of prophets, not for our clay,
and drive men mad by your promised
impossible peace, your harrowing oracles of love;
and how may we walk upon this earth
                                    with forceful human stir
unless we adore you and betray?

HEAR, O ISRAEL

Exiled into the world
you are aliens in it
as Spirit is alien

You are its embodiment
and your travail here
is an unending refutation

For the Cosmos itself framed you
to mock God's pretense
to infinite Justice and Love

THE LYRIC

As moles construct
their burrows
and birds their nests,
the lyric poet
invents his own world

With sunsets and petunias
skylarks
a heart a great love
has cracked

Mine's made
from charred bones,
the smiles of fair-haired
humans
looking at them

WHOM I WRITE FOR

When reading me, I want you to feel
    as if I had ripped your skin off;
Or gouged out your eyes with my fingers;
Or scalped you, and afterwards burnt your hair
    in the staring sockets; having first filled them
with fluid from your son's lighter.
I want you to feel as if I had slammed
    your child's head against a spike;
And cut off your member and stuck it in your
    wife's mouth to smoke like a cigar.

For I do not write to improve your soul;
    or to make you feel better, or more humane;
Nor do I write to give you any new emotions;
Or to make you proud to be able to experience them
    or to recognize them in others.
I leave that to the fraternity of lying poets
    — no prophets, but toadies and trained seals!

How much evil there is in the best of them
    as their envy and impotence flower into poems
And their anality into love of man, into virtue:
Especially when they tell you, sensitively,
    what it feels like to be a potato.

I write for the young man, demented,
    who dropped the bomb on Hiroshima;
I write for Nasser and Ben Gurion;
For Kruschev and President Kennedy;
    for the Defense Secretary
voted forty-six billions for the extirpation
    of humans everywhere.
I write for the Polish officers machine-gunned
    in the Katyn forest;
I write for the gassed, burnt, tortured,
    and humiliated everywhere;

I write for Castro and Tse-tung, the only poets
    I ever learned anything from;
I write for Adolph Eichmann, compliant clerk
    to that madman, the human race;
For his devoted wife and loyal son.

Give me words fierce and jagged enough
    to tear your skin like shrapnel;
Hot and searing enough to fuse
    the flesh off your blackened skeleton;
Words with the sound of crunching bones
or bursting eyeballs;
    or a nose being smashed with a gun butt;
Words with the soft plash of intestines
    falling out of your belly;
Or cruel and sad as the thought which tells you
    "This is the end"
And you feel Time oozing out of your veins
    and yourself becoming one with the weightless dark.

WAGSCHAL EXHIBITION

The Garden of Eden.
              After the Fall
too traumatized to flutter a wing
butterflies and birds drape
the gangrenous vegetation
like monstrous black snowflakes.

Next, our exiled first parents
framed on the adjoining wall.
Clearly the unlooked-for vision of evil
has unhinged them. Note
the sad, mad squint in their eyes.

Now take a hard look at their descendants
whose gift of self-knowledge
makes them insecure, makes them cruel.
Malice and discontent
are the only vital signs they give
they can still be counted alive.

The sour taste of themselves
is manifest on their mouths,
in their unfocused stare.
From them joy long ago has fled.
Living, they are as dead.

The failed violinist.
The self-despising lawyer.
The art teacher, his soft belly
pink and sleek. And
several middle-aged women, a smirk
betraying the dirty secret in their skulls.

Ah, but they are justified.
At the end they are justified.
Once again they enable art
to triumph over nausea.

Don Stewart Art Gallery
Montreal, November 15, 1984

THE BLACK HUNTSMEN

Before ever I knew men were hunting me
I knew delight as water in a glass in a pool;
The childish heart then
Was ears nose eyes twiceten fingers,
And the torpid slum street, in summer,
A cut vein of the sun
That shed goldmotes by the million
Against a boy's bare toe foot ankle knee.

Then when the old year fell out of the window
To break into snowflakes on the cold stones of City Hall
I discovered Tennyson in a secondhand bookstore;
He put his bugle for me to his bearded mouth,
And down his Aquitaine nose a diminutive King Arthur
Rode out of our grocery shop bowing to left and to right,
Bearing my mother's *sheitl* with him;
And for a whole week after that
I called my cat Launcelot.

Now I look out for the evil retinue
Making their sortie out of a forest of gold;
Afterwards their dames shall weave my *tzitzith*
Into a tapestry,
Though for myself I had preferred
A death by water or sky.

THE BENEDICTION

The Sabbath candles
my mother blesses
burn brightly

The flames dance
like little old men,
their visages
crumpled up with joy

To what music?
Or is it the silence
my mother
            has just shut the door on?

Souls are the candleflames'
blue centre
burning stilly;
I gaze entranced
at those of long departed
rabbinical ancestors
lecherous great-uncles
murdered kin
famed disputants in seminaries

Their shadows
linked as one
flicker
on the Friday-white tablecloth

While all the little old men
dance joyfully
in their orbits

THE SEARCH

My father's name was Moses; his beard was black
and black the eyes that beheld God's light;
they never looked upon me but they saw
a crazy imp dropt somehow from the sky
and then I knew from his holy stare
I had disgraced the Prophets and the Law.

Nor was I my mother's prayer;
she who all day railed at a religious indolence
that kept her man warm under his prayershawl
while her reaching arm froze with each customer
who brought a needed penny to her store;
added to another it paid the food and rent.

An ill-matched pair they were. My father
thought he saw Jehovah everywhere,
entertaining his messengers every day
though visible to him alone in that room
where making his fastidious cheese
he dreamt of living in Zion at his ease.

My mother: unpoetical as a pot of clay,
with as much mysticism in her as a banker
or a steward; lamenting God's will for her
yet blessing it with each Friday's candles.
But O her sturdy mind has served me well
who see how humans forge with lies their lonely hell.

Alien and bitter the road my forbears knew:
fugitives forever eating unleavened bread
and hated pariahs because of that one Jew
who taught the tenderest Christian how to hate
and harry them to whatever holes they sped.
Times there were the living envied the dead.

22

Iconoclasts, dreamers, men who stood alone:
Freud and Marx, the great Maimonides
and Spinoza who defied even his own.
In my veins runs their rebellious blood.
I tread with them the selfsame antique road
and seek everywhere the faintest scent of God.

MY FATHER

His voice is low. He leaves behind
The cold, the dross, the hates of men.
He will extol the ways of God
And grow disdainful of the blind.

Of Israel's breed he hums and sings.
He slowly stirs his jaundiced tea
And sighs for lemon . . . ach. His room
Is empty and he talks with kings.

DEATH OF MOISHE LAZAROVITCH

My father's coffin pointed me to this:
O arrogant with new life, his black beard
Fierce and stiff and partner to the dark wood
Sent me the way to what I most had feared.

Became at the last a ring of bright light,
A well whose wall of mourning faces turned
My sighs to silence to a deep wound
Which stained the outstretched figure as it burned.

I swear it burned! If not, why the bright light
Like a tall post that had caught the sun's ray?
White the figure was and bright O so bright,
I have not seen its equal since that day.

I do not know how they lifted him up
Or held the vessel near their mourning silk,
But their going was like a roar of flames
And Matter sang in my ears like poured milk.

ELAN

He phoned, the eldest brother,
To ask about his agèd mother.
"O she does well," I said,
"Though just now her stern is red
with a large ulcer."
"And doesn't that disturb her?"
"No," I quickly replied,
"It's on the opposite side
to one she had a month ago;
This comforts her so.
She says, 'If ulcers can get around,
So can she,' — and stays above the ground."

KEINE LAZAROVITCH: 1870—1959

When I saw my mother's head on the cold pillow,
Her white waterfalling hair in the cheeks' hollows,
I thought, quietly circling my grief, of how
She had loved God but cursed extravagantly his creatures.

For her final mouth was not water but a curse,
A small black hole, a black rent in the universe,
Which damned the green earth, stars and trees in its stillness
And the inescapable lousiness of growing old.

And I record she was comfortless, vituperative,
Ignorant, glad, and much else besides; I believe
She endlessly praised her black eyebrows, their thick weave,
Till plagiarizing Death leaned down and took them for his
        mould.

And spoiled a dignity I shall not again find,
And the fury of her stubborn limited mind:
Now none will shake her amber beads and call God blind,
Or wear them upon a breast so radiantly.

O fierce she was, mean and unaccommodating;
But I think now of the toss of her gold earrings,
Their proud carnal assertion, and her youngest sings
While all the rivers of her red veins move into the sea.

ANTINOMIES

Put a bottle of wine, uncorked, at his elbow,
a bright crystal glass in his hand
and without interrupting him let him speak
of the blasphemous green toilet in the kitchen
mocking the Sabbath candles his mother had blessed;
opposites he thought them like his own parents
who'd engendered him to walk all his life
on awkward legs one shorter than the other
between opposing lines parallel as railway tracks

Halfway down the bottle he'll tell you
his father was a visionary with black eyes, black beard,
who entertained the Lord's angels just as the patriarchs
once had; closing each morning the sanctuary
bedroom door on a scolding wife sullen with grief,
the noisy atheism of trade and an outraged God
too confused by the odours of cotton bags and herrings,
so unlike the smell of sacrificial kine,
to send down his flaming bolts, a merciless plague or two

If you let him finish the bottle, whether
you're listening or not, your unshared thoughts on
the fingernail reddening on the white tablecloth,
he'll say his mind still races between sanctuary
and grocery store, Sabbath candles and toilet
and that even now he sometimes sees his father's angels
slide off the black wicks and spread their wings of smoke
but when he says that, large drops of moisture
form on his lids and brighten his cynical eyes

BURNT OFFERING

When I was a ragged child
alive only with cats and dreams
you'd descend, a fairy princess
remote with charabanc and riches.

Settled in our one comfortable chair
you'd send me out
for your burnt almonds.
How you loved them!

And my errand done,
always, graciously, you dropped a dime
into my moist palm
for a Magnet or Gem.

This morning, the Lord of Israel
sent his angel
to fetch you:
one of his burnt almonds.

Montreal,
March 30, 1985

REQUIEM FOR A. M. KLEIN

They say you keep the devils laughing by your wit
And all the furnaces stilled that they may hear it.

I remember your cigarette-stained fingers
The rimless glasses that glinted with your wit
And the bowtie protruding
Under your chin like a spotted tongue

Your scholar's mind neat as your hair
And the jaunty self-loving complacencies
That made me think of plump pumpkin seeds
Falling from your mouth, the epigrams

I finally gave up counting
Scattering like the pigeons on St. Mark's square
When a piston ring suddenly explodes.
I still wonder at your psychological obtuseness

And the sentimentality each clever Jew
Misconstrues for sensitivity:
Fool's gold which you, O alchemist,
Changed into precious metal, solid and true

Warm-hearted egoist, my dear unforgettable Abe,
You were a medieval troubador
Who somehow wandered into a lawyer's office
And could not find your way back again

Though the reverent adolescent
Like the Virgil which fee-less you taught him
Would have taken your hand and led you out
Muttering the learned hexameters like a charm

Now grey-haired I diet, quarrel with my son,
Watch a young girl make love to herself,

Occasionally speak to God and for your sake
Resolve to listen without irony to young poets

But still muse on your bronzed tits of Justice.
Yes, here where every island has its immortal bard
I think of you with grateful tears and affection
And give them your fresh imperishable name

DOROTHY PARKER
(1893 – 1967)

I read you when I was a younger man;
Your poems, your stories, and your articles;
And recently a sketch that came to hand
Gave me again the fine familiar thrills.

Your mockery was both gay and bitter,
Your revenge on a world that made you sad;
It was your knife for an ancient tumour:
Men being mad, you said that men were mad.

Well, death let you make your jests. Now his own
Has quite surprised you by its calibre
And left you speechless. Goodbye, dear woman.
No more witticisms from you. Alas, no more.

BORIS PASTERNAK

Boris, you were soft as a boiled potato.
No Hemingway, women had you by your balls
all your life though you had the good sense
to stick with two of them to the very end.
     Apartments of your own divided mind,
you craved to have at once passion and order,
adventure and security; the sure bridge
spanning the terrifying chasm below.
Contrary winds turned you like a weathercock.

Was it weakness made you write the gospel poems,
blubbering at the foot of the Cross
where you'd flung yourself — a baptized unheroic Jew?
Pen for an anti-Semitic vodka-swilling boor
     a shifty unforgivable missive
begging him to let you stay in that foul land
where every lout and time-serving scribbler
might fling his dirt at you,
leer as you wiped the filth from your open face?

Maybe the fault lay in your Jewish genes,
in your terrible need to suffer and to please.
Or was it, after all, only the bored indifference
of transcendent genius that moves always
     on the twin rails of here and beyond, the ideal
and actual, but unerringly to that great good place
where Dr. Zhivago opens its welcoming arms
to seer and sod, revolutionist and pharisee,
and poems stay perfect in the mind of God?

OSIP MANDELSTAM
(1891 – 1940)

I once did an hour-long TV show reading
from your *Stamen* and *Tristia;* out there
were my compatriots who had never before
heard of your name and pain, your nightmare fate;
of course the impresario spoke impressively
about your stay in Paris where you mastered
the French symbolists, your skill as translator
(what pre-Belsen Jew hadn't promiscuously
shacked up with five or six gentile cultures?),
the Hellenic feeling in your prose and poems
— to be brief, he filled in the familiar picture
of enlightened Jew, ass bared to the winds

But when that self-taught master symbolist
il miglior fabbro put you on his list of touchables
that was the end; you perished in the land waste
of Siberia, precisely where no one knows and few care,
for in that stinking *imperium* whose literature
you adorned like a surreal Star of David
you're still an unclaimed name, a Jewish ghost
who wanders occasionally into enclaves
of forlorn intellectuals listening
for the ironic scrape of your voice
in the subversive hum of underground presses

I know my fellow Canadians, Osip;
they forgot your name and fate as swiftly
as they learned them, switching off
the contorted image of pain with their sets,
choosing a glass darkness to one which starting
in the mind covers the earth in permanent eclipse;
so they chew branflakes and crabmeat, gossip, make love,
take out insurance against fires and death
while our poetesses explore their depressions
in delicate complaints regular as menstruation

34

or eviscerate a dead god for metaphors;
the men-poets displaying codpieces of wampum,
the safer legends of prairie Indian and Eskimo

Under a sour and birdless heaven
TV crosses stretch across a flat Calvary
and plaza storewindows give me
the blank expressionless stare of imbeciles:
this is Toronto, not St. Petersburg on the Neva;
though seas, death and silent decades separate us
we yet speak to each other, brother to brother;
your forgotten martyrdom has taught me scorn
for hassidic world-savers without guns and tanks:
they are mankind's gold and ivory toilet bowls
where brute or dictator relieves himself
when reading their grave messages to posterity
— let us be the rapturous eye of the hurricane
flashing the Jew's will, his mocking contempt for slaves

FOR NADEZHDA MANDELSTAM

Nadezhda, my grey-haired love, my wrinkled darling
I write you from the cold whiteness of Toronto
Hoping my affection for you thaws the ice and snow
Between us, melts the barbed wire around your heart.

Tough gallant lady, you're so much like my mother.
She too would have spat at the Kremlin's mountaineer,
At the contemptible pygmies and half-men who let him
Play tunes on their skulls with his grubby fingers.

I've friends with soft hearts and softer heads
Who grieve when fire rains down on evil men
And perhaps you also see the bulging eyes of the dead
And feel the stink and silence that surrounds them

As they move into history. Perhaps like them
You also march in groups, sign petitions, disapprove
Of America's might, saying what message has poetry
For this sad demented world except love.

Perhaps. But not I, my grey-haired darling.
When freedom flings his fiery horseshoes they explode,
Sending scorching nails with a loud noise
At the heads, eyes and groins of my enemies.

In a hard school it was drilled into me
To tumble vermin into a hot cauldron death;
In the dungheap of contemporary history
The Stalins hatch everywhere. The poet must break

Their backs with a hammer's blow.
One does not fool around with broad-chested Ossetes.
One does not wait to see their cockroach whiskers grow.
Were Osip with us he'd have my sad ache and agree.

HEINRICH HEINE

I dreamt that I was Satan
Being warmed by molten stones
And critics who had scorned me
Had to memorize my poems

As pious Jews read their Scroll
Book to book the year around
They recite my brilliant lines;
Not a bad one can they find

To reclaim their wizened souls,
Day in day out till time ends
They sing my deathless *Lieder*
And dance on these blazing coals

MRS. FORNHEIM, REFUGEE

Very merciful was the cancer
Which first blinding you altogether
Afterwards stopped up your hearing;
At the end when Death was nearing,
Black-gloved, to gather you in
You did not demur, or fear
One you could not see or hear.

I taught you Shakespeare's tongue, not knowing
The time and manner of your going;
Certainly if with ghosts to dwell,
German would have served as well.
Voyaging lady, I wish for you
An Englishwoman to talk to,
An unruffled listener,
And green words to say to her.

THE IMPROVED BINOCULARS

Below me the city was in flames:
the firemen were the first to save
themselves. I saw steeples fall on their knees.

I saw an agent kick the charred bodies
from an orphanage to one side, marking
the site carefully for a future speculation.

Lovers stopped short of the final spasm
and went off angrily in opposite directions,
their elbows held by giant escorts of fire.

Then the dignitaries rode across the bridges
under an auricle of light which delighted them,
noting for later punishment those that went before.

And the rest of the populace, their mouths
distorted by an unusual gladness, bawled thanks
to this comely and ravaging ally, asking

Only for more light with which to see
their neighbour's destruction.

All this I saw through my improved binoculars.

INCIDENT AT THE CATHEDRAL

Your hands, Jeshua, were stretched out
in welcome
and weren't it for a couple of rusty nails
I think you would have embraced me
so glad were you to see one of your kin

But you observed — didn't you? —
how the guard chased me out
because my bare knees were showing;
he thought you'd be angry
and your mother too,
in fact the entire *mishpoche*
if I walked in wearing khaki shorts

Sometimes, brother Jeshua, I wonder
whether you know
what imbecilities have been said and done
in your name, what madnesses

At other times, though,
seeing you hanging so helplessly
on the Cross
with that agonized look on your face
I know as if you had spoken that you know

Barcelona,
August 1, 1975

40

FOR MY BROTHER JESUS

My father had terrible words for you
— whoreson, bastard, *meshumad;*
and my mother loosed Yiddish curses
on your name and the devil's spawn
on their way to church
that scraped the frosted horsebuns
from the wintry Montreal street
to fling clattering into our passageway

Did you ever hear an angered
Jewish woman curse? Never mind the words:
at the intonation alone, Jesus,
the rusted nails would drop out
from your pierced hands and feet
and scatter to the four ends of the earth

Luckless man, at least
that much you were spared

In my family you
were a *mamzer,* a *yoshke pondrik*
and main reason for their affliction and pain.
Even now I see the contemptuous curl
on my gentle father's lips;
my mother's never-ending singsong curses
still ring in my ears more loud
than the bells I heard each Sunday morning,
their clappers darkening the outside air

Priests and nuns
were black blots on the snow
— forbidding birds, crows

Up there
up there beside the Good Old Man
we invented and the lyring angels

do you get the picture, my hapless brother:
deserted daily, hourly
by the Philistines you hoped to save
and the murdering heathens,
your own victimized kin hating and despising
you?

O crucified poet
your agonized face haunts me
as it did when I was a boy;
I follow your strange figure
through all the crooked passageways
of history, the walls reverberating
with ironic whisperings and cries,
the unending sound of cannon fire
and rending groans, the clatter
of blood-soaked swords falling
on armour and stone
to lose you finally among your excited brethren
haranguing and haloing them
with your words of love,
your voice gentle as my father's

42

THE SIGN OF THE CROSS

Assuredly, my brothers, not a symbol
of impotence and failure
nor of humiliation and defeat

But of spiritual power, forever
beyond the reach of nails or bullets,
tanks and bombers

Of the eternal Jew crucified
for freedom and creativity

And recalling to despots everywhere
how the Roman eagles moulted and died
In hoc signo vinces

MAGDALENA

Not you, brother; a crack-brained whore
from whom seven devils rushed out
founded the Christian religion:
though stone dead you appeared to her
and she cried out, "He has risen!"

Our famed ancestor, Joshua,
with a clarion blare of trumpets
put sinful Jericho to rout:
she swept the Eagles from the sky
with one wild hysterical shout

THE SINNER

Arrogantly I cursed the fig tree
the scribes and pharisees,
my eyes flashing with fierce certitude
my voice made confident by rage.

"We are God's children," I shouted
at my simple hearers
and won them over with bribes of loaves and fishes
a spate of dazzling miracles.

The dead talked, the palsied walked;
the circumcised, their ringlets shaking, roared
each time I tripped up rabbi and sage:
my smile was passed around by my disciples.

"You who are sinless, hurl the first stone!"
My own tongue had formed those words,
my own sweet self, wiser than Gamaliel's.
My frame shook with the thought of my uniqueness.

And perceiving the pride I loathed uncoil itself
I stomped on its grinning mouth; only to see the viper
flee from my heel, swift with my own triumphant cry.
There was no breakout from the imprisoning self.

Till my enemies seized me one terrible night
and bound me fast and dying to a cross.
Then godlike with bitter self-knowledge and sinless
only with my last groan did I give up my pride.

THE CRUCIFIXION

Every unbelieving Jew
puts another nail in our Lord's cross;
you're all guilty for his death
each one of you, now and always

So the young Anglican priest told me,
fresh out of the seminary
his features clean-cut but severe
and his frank Anglo-Saxon eyes loving and clear

I asked him: Is Yehudi Menuhin also guilty?
Jack Benny? Abzug? Chagall? Me too?
With gloomy conviction he replied, All,
Christ's death is on every Jew

At least I'm in good company, I said
with Spinoza Freud Disraeli Gertrude Stein
and the immortal Einstein:
a great band of murderers if you count living and dead

Where could be found one more illustrious
or is the death of Socrates on all Greeks
and that of poor Joan on all Englishmen?
Ah, no, said the Anglican priest loving and meek

That's another matter. Certainly. But of course. Quite.
He was firm and though aroused still polite;
and it came to me in a flash: civilizations
like topsoil worms nurture sadists

Degenerate scum, refuse,
the enslaved cripples on whom culture rests;
the maimed and ill need one weaker than
        themselves to scourge
— not Jeshua but each racked Jew is on that Cross!

THE GALILEAN

Only for one sickening moment
the houses and the hills of Jerusalem
blur into a pain dull as nausea,
clearing into steel-sharp agonizing focus
as he feels the wet corroding salt
leak down his death-pale cheeks and beard
and his dying senses track the guiltless insect
making a noisome halo around his head

Past houses, past barren outlying hill
there's nothing for his eyes to see . . . nothing;
and nothing is in the red folds of the sky,
no Father's voice to call or comfort him
though they'd raised him high enough to hear it;
only the demented noise of the insect
and below that, the Roman soldiers
dicing loudly for his mud-bespattered garments

Though no one had forsaken him, he is lost;
mistaken and lost, and dying for an absurdity:
for a dream, a fairytale, an illusion.
Still, he's not embittered; though bound, he's free,
free at last from hope and self-deception.
An instant before he gave up his ghost
he'd have wiped the troubling mist from his eyes
but the stranger's hands were nailed fast to the cross

THE TRUE PICTURE

Jeshua
the *goyim* everywhere on this planet
see you in their own likeness

In England they limn you
as fair-haired Briton genteel as tea;
in Singapore and Hong Kong
your eyes are wise and slanted
and here on the island of Lesbos
you look as Greek as Theodorakis,
your hair sleeked down with olive oil

In France you are a hollow-cheeked Voltairean
and I've seen you look down on Germans
like an earnest schoolmaster
asking the conjugation
for the Latin verb *exterminare*

Brother, if it's the last thing I do
in this rotten beautiful world
I'm going to paint you
with your white robe parted
and your circumcised cock showing
caught in the fringes
of your *talith*

XIANITY

Brother and fellow poet,
is this what you wanted?

The mutterings of bead-counting hysterics?
The snufflings of joyless misfits and cripples
fearful of death, more fearful of life?
The *misereres* of the doomed dregs
in every large metropolis of the world?
The hosannahs of the conformist hordes
stinking of money and respectability?

Is this what you wanted:
the grey suburban church and the greyer people
shambling into it each Sunday
you who openly consorted with whores and drunkards
and so loved laughter and joy
that you were willing to be crucified for them?

SHLEMIHL

Your words were not meant for *goyim*,
for necrophiles and ill-natured scum:
for the forever damaged humans
sloth and impotency have made vindictive.

Joyous people should have heard your *meshalim*,
only those who glow with an inner fire
and need neither possessions nor fame
to achieve an illusion of abundance.

In century after century
the gentiles have poured your rich blood
into their boredom and futility:
it soothed them between their reeking infamies.

Shlemihl! You should have preached only
to the converted, the happy extravagant few
and left the fierce cripples of the world
to smash their crutches on one another's heads.

Montreal,
November 8, 1978

50

THE LUMINOUS BAGEL

Not only did a loony whore
from whom earlier
seven devils had rushed out
have a vision of Jesus,
and Simon Cephas the Fickle
misnamed the Rock
who saw him face to face
in Galilee
after the crucifixion,
and James and Paul

My friends, I speak the truth:
he appeared to me also
one day when I was standing
on the steps of an Anglican church
(I wasn't born circumcised for nothing)
and hailing me as if
we'd had the same pock-marked rabbi
on St. Elizabeth Street
said, pointing to the closed doors:
"*Yisroel*, what do those elegant WASPS
in there
say about me?"

I was frightened but I replied,
"That you're the Son of God, Jeshua,
and that you asked to be crucified
in remission of their sins."

"*Mishegoyim*," he muttered aloud
in surprisingly clear Yiddish
and hastily re-mounting his moped
disappeared into the traffic,
leaving me his halo
to twirl around my finger
like a luminous bagel

JESHUA

Brother, I've seen you worshipped in Bangkok
And your imagined likeness in Seoul
Where muttering slant-eyed Chinese women
Light candles for your tortured Jewish soul.

How on earth did you do it, Jesus?
Of course you had the Orphic qualities
Of grace and passion, a human bearing
That won all hearts at once (no, not all;
The Roman puppets skulked and hated you
As did the pious quislings in their pay)
Also, there was the greater poet Isaiah
From whom you cribbed most of what you had to say,
And Amos and fierce-eyed Jeremiah.
Still, you added some goodness of your own,
A fervour about love, a certain tone
And long before the paroles of Saint Nietzsche
(Holy infidel) you put the saved man
In that bright space beyond good and evil.

Yet how on earth did it ever happen?
Was it Saul, that Greek-speaking Hebrew sod?
The mendacious gospels and Church Fathers
Whose tender words sired pillage and ruin?
The pious rabble for whom your "good news"
Meant the maiming and burning of Jews,
Their dark skins sizzling in the Christian fires?
The knee-jerkings and castrati choirs?
Or was it the boring Sunday sermon
Drove out of their wits Spaniard and German
Who, one using gas and the other flame,
Proved the effulgent power of your Name?
Ah, your Sonship has driven quite batty
Priests and popes and Europe's culturati.

I'm stymied. How could they do it to you,
A life-loving, feasting, quick-witted Jew
Who like myself and my cousin Heinrich
Dangled between your legs a Jewish prick?
Was it then the over-refined women
Who must have a god to adore and kiss
And are at peace thinking you and your Dad
Transcend whatever is imperfect, bad
Viz., that unlike the husbands they know
Immortal gods never break wind or piss
And that some chartered rib-tickling devil
Stuck your smooth limbs with balls and genital?

Come back, long-lost brother, come back to us.
Turn away from the scrofulous paintings
By sick Europeans who have limned you
As French, Italian, Polack, and German
Or — foul parody — fair-haired Englishman
But never as sane exuberant Jew.
Leave behind you the stink of incense, groans
Prostrations, prayers, homilies, and moans
Now rising in a thousand languages
Not counting Swahili and Javanese.
Like maggots in a corse, lies breeding lies.
Breeding impotence and hypocrisy,
The neurotic hang-up with tombs and death,
Blood gouts, the *santon's* malodorous breath
— Ghoulishness discharging the cattle-car
Into the bloody hole of Babi Yar.
For the little children you wished to save
Gentile Europe found the covering mass grave,
Beside the Church to which you gave your name
The bodies of murdered Jews dissolve in lime.

Dear passionate man, Jeshua-Jesus,
Wipe your fine Hebrew nose on the cultus
That fatal as cancer spreads far and wide
Wherever prole and sick bourgeois abide;
The discontented, crippled, ill-at-ease
That to your image yowl and bend their knees,
The tools and half-men of a brassy age
Who smile and fawn because they dare not rage.
Tell them 'twas brother Saul's cloddish mistake;
To burn all altars and all sceptres break
And when the *pappas* swings his thurible
To spin him round and send him off to Hell;
Then taking forgiveness from the wronged Jew
Mocked and scourged by your hate-filled retinue
To look up at the white-blue sun-glowing sky
And hail new dawns with an exulting cry.

Athens,
June 23, 1975

54

JESUS AND SAINT PAUL

I curse you, Saul of Tarsus.
I curse you as once I cursed a barren fig tree.
My name was Jeshua, not Jesus;
Not God's Son but a Hebrew revolutionary
I stirred up rebellion till the Romans crucified me.

I curse you, Saul of Tarsus.
I curse you, O epileptic Hellenized sod
And the vile dolts who call me Jesus;
Who bowing to me as the third part of their god
Have scourged the seed of Abraham with fire and sword
    and rod.

I curse you, Saul of Tarsus.
I curse you as once I cursed the rich Pharisee.
For I who preached God's love and justice
Who brought the glad tidings to make Jew and Roman free
See how from your sick converts my people must hide
    and flee.

CONVERSOS

With their genius
they inscribed the most dazzling page
in Spanish civilization
— the sixteenth century.

Those others, the wretched Jews
who chose death over baptism,
illumined the heavy darkness only
for as long as they burned to ash.

"All the heresies of Europe
are sown by the descendants of Jews,"
someone records Philip II as saying.

History is a tragicomedian:
in the arteries of the persecuting king
ran the blood of Conversos.

THE GOLDEN AGE OF SPANISH PAINTING

Pietàs and Assumptions, Virgins and Saints:
Someone has worked hard to put these lies on the wall.
I'll laugh in three colours at their display
And with my sneezings blow away false paint.
El Greco, Murillo, Velázquez, Zurbarán:
Fine Christian gentlemen were they all, I feel;
But did they *never* see an *auto-da-fé*
Or a Jew broken for his faith on a wheel?

Royal Academy of Fine Arts
London, February 10, 1976

ON SEEING THE STATUETTES OF EZEKIEL AND JEREMIAH IN THE CHURCH OF NOTRE DAME

They have given you French names
    and made you captive, my rugged
troublesome compatriots;
    your splendid beards, here, are epicene,
plaster white
        and your angers
unclothed with Palestinian hills quite lost
in this immense and ugly edifice.

You are bored — I see it — sultry prophets
    with priests and nuns
(What coarse jokes must pass between you!)
    and with those morbidly religious
i.e. my prize brother-in-law
              ex-Lawrencian
pawing his rosary, and his wife
sick with many guilts.

Believe me I would gladly take you
    from this spidery church
its bad melodrama, its musty smell of candle
    and set you both free again
in no make-believe world
        of sin and penitence
but the sunlit square opposite
alive at noon with arrogant men.

Yet cheer up Ezekiel and you Jeremiah
    who were once cast into a pit;

I shall not leave you here incensed, uneasy
        among alien Catholic saints
but shall bring you from time to time
                my hot Hebrew heart
as passionate as your own, and stand
with you here awhile in aching confraternity.

SAINT PINCHAS

You sit bolt upright as if you want to know
Why so many crowd to kiss your Jewish toe;
Why gaunt acolytes, why prelates wearing stoles
Rub their pious hairdos under your worn-out sole
And all file reverently before your feet
To move their hungering lips as if they would eat
While in every procession the more devout
Struggle to finger the metal toe-jam out.
Kissing or smelling the stale dust they press
A breezy crucifix and bowing low bless
The gold air around them, themselves most of all,
Grateful they have not fallen despite the Fall.
Pinchas, your rubbed, much-patted, much-smacked toes shine
With a radiance your brother made divine
Though to kindred Jews it seems the big one glows
Bright and secular like W. C. Fields' nose
And if you could would at once raise it to poke
The eyes out of these stupid credulous folk
And with Jewish sardony plant a neat kick
In the wet mouth of that black-gowned tonsured wick
Who scans my girl when he's left off kissing your toe
As if he'd like to sport with her an hour or so,
Make in his confessional the two-backed beast
Chomp on her nipples and on her vulva feast.
The dumbfounded expression on your face
Here in this basilica seems quite in place
As though it was wanting all your brazen art
To stiffly sit on a wild redundant fart
So propelling it might make your figure rise
Before their delighted superstitious eyes:
My dear silly Pinchas, stunned you look as though
You had heard again the cock's first rending crow.

Saint Peter's Basilica,
June 4, 1975

60

THIS MACHINE AGE

For fifteen cents,
the label read,
the Virgin's halo
would light up
for three minutes.
The man dropped
the pieces of money
into the machine's slot
and looked about
the vast, gloomy church
empty except
for him and me.
When his gaze came back
to the halo
it was still unlit
— a dark infuriating zero.

He gave the machine
a careful kick
to bring the lights
of the circle on.
It didn't.
"Damn it!" he shouted,
"Why doesn't it light up?"
He kicked again
and muttered something
I didn't hear.
But I could guess
from the way he looked
he thought divine sereneness
a poker-faced fraud
and himself taken in
by the Mother of God.

KING KONG

An immense gas tank
pinions the giant ape.
O they've nailed him this time!

For mockery
the depleted half-men
have fixed a silverfoil crown
upon his head

At the end,
one whom great love had betrayed
he lies heavy and dead on the ground
while the frantic hordes,
flashbulbs popping light
above the passionate faces,
take pictures
of his big exposed heart
now bleeding for all of them
into their sensitive whirring cameras

TERRORISTS

Insulted, forsaken exiles
harried, harassed, shat on
learning
      Justice is heard only
when it speaks through the mouth
of a cannon

learning
      Right lies waiting
to fly out of a gun barrel

learning weakness is the one crime
history never pardons or condones

Uselessly you bruise yourselves, squirming
against civilization's whipping post;
Black September wolfcubs
terrify only themselves

The Jewish terrorists, ah:
Maimonides, Spinoza, Freud,
Marx

The whole world is still quaking

C'EST FINI

Three Jews, three Jews
    lit a fuse
    under the bum
    of Christendom

See how Jack comes tumbling down

Whee . . .

First, Baruch Spinoza
    who mixing Ethics with Euclid
    dropped the lid
    on the Christ myth;
    though pope and priest strain
    they'll never lift open that lid again

Whee . . .

Then from across the Rhine
    hopping mad came Marx
    whose black beard shook
    whose fierce eyes rolled
    as his carbuncles explained
    how Christian gentlemen got their gold

Whee . . .

Lastly, the chief subversive of all:
    listen, my dear friends, where Freud is
    the Austro-Hungarian Empire is no more
    — nor the German either

Whee . . .

Three Jews, three Jews
 lit a fuse
 under the bum
 of bourgeois Christendom;
 it's done for, it's had its day;
 three Jews chomping on cigars
 puffed it away

Whee . . .

A BRIEF HISTORY OF THE JEWS

So what if you gave the world
Spinoza and Marx, Freud and Einstein,
as well as scores of its most famous
statesmen and healers

Not to mention
painters, poets, musicians
and the saner portions
of Christianity and Islamism

The ungrateful swine
will still burn you in ovens
if envy and baseness are strong enough
and they can invent the necessary excuses

My obstinate brothers
no one was humanized
by your sublime follies
except yourselves!

IBN GABRIOL

You ask me
    "What is a Jew?"

One of Abraham's seed
participating
    in an eternal colloquy
concerning the nature
of God and Man

While the others
    when not louts
or murderers
holding up the discussion
    with blows and shouts

Stand around and listen

THE MAGICIAN

Europe's most civilized minds, brilliant and sick
— Eliot, Pound, Yeats, and Wyndham Lewis,
Hauptmann and Hamsun, Céline and Benn.
The Jew changed them all into sputtering wicks
More coarse and benighted than the Russian *moujik*.

CAIN

Taking the air rifle from my son's hand,
I measured back five paces, the Hebrew
In me, narcissist, father of children,
Laid to rest. From there I took aim and fired.
The silent ball hit the frog's back an inch
Below the head. He jumped at the surprise
Of it, suddenly tickled or startled
(He must have thought) and leaped from the wet sand
Into the surrounding brown water. But
The ball had done its mischief. His next spring
Was a miserable flop, the thrust all gone
Out of his legs. He tried — like Bruce — again,
Throwing out his sensitive pianist's
Hands as a dwarf might or a helpless child.
His splash disturbed the quiet pondwater
And one old frog behind his weedy moat
Blinking, looking self-complacently on.
The linn's surface at once became closing
Eyelids and bubbles like notes of music
Liquid, luminous, dropping from the page
White, white-bearded, a rapid crescendo
Of inaudible sounds and a crone's whispering
Backstage among the reeds and bulrushes
As for an expiring Lear or Oedipus.

But Death makes us all look ridiculous.
Consider this frog (dog, hog, what you will)
Sprawling, his absurd corpse rocked by the tides
That his last vain spring had set in movement.
Like a retired oldster, I couldn't help sneer,
Living off the last of his insurance:
Billows — now crumbling — the premiums paid.
Absurd, how absurd. I wanted to kill
At the mockery of it, kill and kill
Again — the self-infatuate frog, dog, hog,
Anything with the stir of life in it,

69

Seeing the dead leaper, Chaplin-footed,
Rocked and cradled in this afternoon
Of tranquil water, reeds, and blazing sun,
The hole in his back clearly visible
And the torn skin a blob of shadow
Moving when the quiet pondwater moved.
O Egypt, marbled Greece, resplendent Rome,
Did you also finally perish from a small bore
In your back you could not scratch? And would
Your mouths open ghostily, gasping out
Among the murky reeds, the hidden frogs,
We climb with crushed spines toward the heavens?

When the next morning I came the same way
The frog was on his back, one delicate
Hand on his belly, and his white shirt front
Spotless. He looked as if he might have been
A comic; tapdancer apologizing
For a fall, or an emcee, his wide grin
Coaxing a laugh from us for an aside
Or perhaps a joke we didn't quite hear.

THE LESSON

This is a finger
This is an eye

Even a small cut causes pain, afterwards soreness;
the terror comes when a bone-shattering bullet
enters the neck, the groin
or the blood rushes after the retreating knife

The thought of death,
of being suddenly reduced to nothing,
makes the lips go white

You must say to yourself
this is not film, this is real
and it's happening to a man
who was once an infant and cried in the dark

Those are real intestines
spilling out into his hand;
the pain and terror are real

Let's begin again
This is a finger
This is an eye

FOR JESUS CHRIST

It began with delicate religious *frissons*
at the blinding of a young Jewess
who incautiously turned away her gaze
from your paraded likeness at Easter.

One pontiff invented the ghetto;
more tender and loving, another commanded
shivering ghosts to wear out its cobblestones
warmed by the yellow star of David.

Having mutilated under your mild forgiving eyes
your idol-hating brothers and sisters,
both peasant and duke knew the joys of penitence,
the ecstatic remorse in sinning flesh.

Your stoutest, most selfless partisans in Europe
laboured nearly two thousand years
to twist your Cross into the Swastika
that tore into our flesh like a fish-hook.

GOTHIC LANDSCAPE

They stand like penitential Augustines
These trees; and in my Jewboy mind they are monks,
Brown-robed, fearful after their long sleep in dungeons;
When I was a child one of them nearly caught me,
But I escaped, tunnelling the snow to my mother's face;
Under her grey shawl I saw God's Assyrian beard,
And a page of *lameds* racing towards me like ostriches.

I've taken no vow not to forget
The torquemadas stirring in the frosty veins:
But the cloister bells deafen me with insults,
And sallow-faced acolytes inform
The snowdrifts what to whisper against me;
Autos-da-fé make red the immaculate sky;
Come soon, O bright Tudor sun!
I do not like this monastic whiteness of winter —
It is a Christ drained of all blood.

THE SABBATH

Each day in our semi-slum house
We fought a battle with cockroaches and rats.
It was a draw, i.e., they ate, so did we.
On Saturday they respected our Sabbath.

Or so it seemed to me, a dreaming boy.
It could've been my father's black beard
More magisterial on that day than weekdays.
Whatever the reason, no rat or roach stirred.

Spotless were parlour and kitchen and bedroom;
My mother's hands had left no speck or crumb.
The plates in the immaculate cupboard glistened:
Perhaps the vermin had been struck dumb.

God's promised peace was in every corner;
After *tophet* there came blessed relief.
Nothing moved on walls or floors. I went outside
And heard the militant shrieks, *"Maudit Juif!"*

SURVIVOR

If at first it disgusts you
be a man: don't give up, don't despair
in this as in most things
habit and practice make perfect

In the beginning try only
for small effects, small incisions
leave the big spurts
for a later period

Start by imagining
an eyeball in your hand
intact as yet, still warm
now put its fellow beside it

In the beginning was the deed:
give yourself a year, no more
to have real eyeballs in your hand
make sure you wipe the blade clean afterward

Continue to read poems
and to enjoy wit in conversation
motto for our times: cultivate your tastes
but deaden your senses

At the beginning if you're careless
feelings may trip you up
you must unlearn tenderness and compassion
above all, compassion

Let all your reveries be of charred bodies
of smashed blue faces
it's not simple
but it's not that difficult either

FOR ERICH MUHSAM

You adored poetry and music.

Ulrich adored parades, uniforms and Bavarian beer.

You dreamed of the perfect social order
where all lived free and caring.

He dreamt of whores and promotions.

You stretched his language through image and metaphor.

He was satisfied with his simple *heils*.

You loved humanity with a passion.

He loved Deutschland Uber Alles, maybe a stray mongrel
or cat.

You revered Jesus, the Jew who came from Nazareth
that the poor might be happy.

He worshipped the antichrist in *Lederhosen*.

Your most wonderful thoughts
had for their goal his happiness and well-being.

You made him happy when he knocked out your teeth
and your right ear hung like "a giant blister
of blood and pus" from his beatings.

You cheerfully gave your life that another might live.

A helper of death, he wore the dreaded insignia
of skull-and-crossbones on his hat.

Unquestionably you possessed genius, an incandescent
mind.

Yes, but an Ulrich has a fist as big as your face.

REINGEMACHT

Why are the birds flying overhead?
Do they make out the waves to be rotting heads?
Do they smell black carrion drifting on the sea?
The midday sun is in the sky,
throwing down his small silver horseshoes
that land near the bobbing heads and floating corpses.
The dog that was friendly yesterday
frantically scoops the sand with his forepaws
as if he were thirstily digging for water
and covers my books and papers with it. He never stops.
I notice a mysterious swarm of flies
where the children are building castles and moats.
A small boat chugs past. A water-skier
alights suddenly as if from nowhere
like an angel come to warn us. Of what?
I fear the worst, brothers and friends.
The calm sea, the blue sky, the laughing children
are deceptions. I tell you I smell burning wood.
I see and hear sizzling flesh, the hissing oils and fats
start fires in the streets.
Tall buildings sway and totter like old men
before they crumble into a waterfall of bricks.
The cries and moans never cease.
The cities of the plain are burning.
London. Berlin. Vienna. Warsaw. Moscow.
Night after night, they blaze like enormous faggots
against the lowering sky.
A hideous smell of gas covers Europe from end to end.
When the cities have burned themselves out
the heavens will open up
and black torrential rains will descend for forty days
and forty nights.
Everything alive is submerged and drowned.
I see no tossing ark.

FOR MY NEIGHBOURS IN HELL

Hate, your adrenalin,
the frenzies of killing and sex
purge your souls of phlegm

Wired up by instincts
at odds with one another,
you are reptiles with a conscience

Only one certain thing life allows:
the long slow suicide
through sloth and conformity

Knowingly, on clean sheets
you breed cadavers
and name the horror "love"

A time-bomb ticks in each of you;
you will self-destruct
when you least want it to happen

Even Lucifer weeps
when he sees you, pale and dazed,
in the sulphurous glow of his furnaces

Your cries of torment
are what keep the Almighty
from hearing his sobs

PROPER READING LIGHT

"You don't understand, my son;
they made lampshades
that they might read
the text better."

"Which text, father?"

"'Love one another.'"

CABALIST

Always his eyes radiated light:
His gentle voice stirred love and hope
God was a Presence that he could touch,
The mental source of an inner might.
For all that, witless humans seized him
And changed him into a bar of soap.

THE INTERLOPER

He went around singing
his fool head off,
stirring their latent evil impulses

They warned him
to stick to ghettos and crematoria
where he might sing for chosen people

He'd be left alone, they said
so long as he didn't disturb the populace
with his joy

Since he persisted in hymning God and Life
what else could they do
but murder him?

ENTRY

He was a Jew
with a faked identity card;
the ghetto was in flames, its puny defenders
scattered, dead

As he crossed the emptied square of the now
silent city
and looking up saw the great
black cathedral of Warsaw
the immoveable stars overhead
he was caught suddenly
in the murderous crossfire of Nazi and partisan guns

He hugged the bloodstained rubbish and stones
and laughed into the dark at how
an impersonal death by a willed or stray bullet
made one at last a human among humans

THE SUBVERSIVE

Just imagine
if Hitler had ordered
the destruction
of all dogs and cats:
the opposition
would have been honourable,
long and unrelenting

Alas, the wicked man
called for volunteers
to exterminate Jews
and christian Europe
went up in smoke,
in a chimney stink
no wind will ever freshen

AT THE BELSEN MEMORIAL

It would be a lie
to say I heard screams
I heard nothing
It would be a lie
to say I saw ribs
like the bones
of beached ships
I saw nothing
It would be a lie
to say I sniffed
the odours
of decomposing crystals
or of bodies
that are left to lie
in the wind and rain
I sniffed nothing
nothing at all
It would be a lie
to say
emaciated ghosts
of little children
brushed against me
and that I reached out
my hands
to touch them
There were no emaciated
ghosts
and my hands
remained in the pockets
of the summer suit
I was wearing
The taste of death
was on my tongue
on my tongue only

When it pierced my neck
I was turned into stone
towering and black
Come:
read the inscription

FOR HANS, MAYBE KLAUS OR TADEUSZ

Who clubbed emaciated men to death

Who machine-gunned old men and women

Who all in the day's work
gassed thousands of humans
and afterwards walked thoughtfully home
to wife and children

Who smashed in the skulls of infants

And is now not a little pleased
with himself, having somehow survived
when so many others died
— so many better ones too

And would do it all over again
if only history offered the chance again
and your beastly arthritis
wasn't acting up
or the old pumper thumping so fast. Right?

Of course you would! Because, really,
life was never so dizzying as then.
How full of surprises each day was.
Though the sausages and good wines
have been plentiful, a glory
has departed from the world.
Dullness has come back again

Let's be up front about this.
For the squashed and depleted
there's no greater happiness
than wiping out another mortal
or humiliating him. Little man,

at last you've made it into history.
In the constellation of human
possibilities, your place is more fixed
than that of Socrates or Christ

From here on you're the reality
by which everything must be weighed
and tested. Haven't you noticed?
Everyone lives as if Auschwitz never happened.

NO WILD DOG

I tell my class
What man can do
No cobra can
And no wild dog

Or other kinds
Of vicious beast:
The prowling wolf
And the mongoose.

I'm told they hate
The smell of gas
And run from fires;
But that's not it

No, that's not it.
It takes reason
And spirit too
Which man alone

Evolved in time
So he can do
The amazing things
No cobra can

And no wild dog.

MAIMONIDEAN PERPLEXITY

Strong in cunning
and implacably cruel

Man slays his kind,
kills them without pity or remorse

Yet their numbers increase
till they cover the earth

Miracle, O Lord,
or Shaitan's enduring love and concern?

THE DARK UNDERSIDE

My animals play. They devour the innards of fish,
then jump, romp, attack the air with their paws
and with fiercest catsnarls, their claws sheathed,
wage mock combats for my Roman pleasure.

But man consumes trophies, ingests the souls
of battered men, the agonies of women and children
to energize his pathetic strut across
the wreathed trap-door that opens on the grave.

The sinister underside of every culture,
his cruelty is no less an exuberance,
a defiance of evil and unbearable pain:
his elixir of life is the blood of the slain.

No matter whose smile he seeks, Dionysus's or Christ's,
he's never more pitiable and terrifying
than when he clears his throat to crow
over the pulped bones of his imagined foe.

DIVINE IMAGE

Swiftly darting in the setting light,
The doomed sparrow feels the falcon's wings.
How beautiful are they both in flight.

THE GRAVEYARD

Lord, I understand the plan, the news is out:
I kill him, he kills me, change and change about,
And you ever in the right; and no wonder
Since it's no great matter who's up, who's under.
Teuton or Slav, Arab or suffering Jew —
Nature, Justice, God — they are all one to you.
The lion breeds the lamb and the antelope
As evil breeds good; darkness, light; despair, hope.

And though your scheme confounds the theologian's wits
All come and go sired by the opposites;
And they decree: He who slays and he who's slain
Leave on your excellent world no crimson stain.
The tragic, warring creatures that here have breath
Are reconciled in the partnership of death;
And death's akin to art, and artists please
To the measure they have stilled the contraries.

Energy must crackle on a silent urn,
Nothing catch fire though Jerusalem burn,
And the lion poised on the poor bok to spring
Hold in his furious jaws no suffering.
Motion and rest, love and hate, heaven and hell
Here cease their Punch-and-Judy show. All is well.
There is no pain in the graveyard or the voice
Whispering in the tombstones: "Rejoice, rejoice."

ETERNAL RECURRENCE

The sleepwalkers are advancing on Armageddon
where the lines form for the final conflict;
they all smile beatifically over
their shopping bags, their hands covered
by diamonds and fresh blood.
A few dash into the fray still wet
from their pools and surfing. Finally,
after the last shriek has died away
the smoke clears over another Stone Age,
over cave dwellers and humans with painted skins:
cannibals devour each other's kidneys and brains.

Another Megiddo rises, another Troy. Again
satyrs link tails and dance in the moonlight;
another Abram hears injunctions the wind utters
or a tapestry fluttering against a wall
and forthwith quits the valley of his forefathers
to begin the tragic husking of mankind,
the reformation of a brute universe
in all its parts by sentience and love;
always his heirs will climb towards the same ruin
until this creation becomes one vast inertness
with not a single mind to know its doom.

THE PREDATOR

The little fox
was lying in a pool of blood,
having gnawed his way out to freedom.

Or the farmhand,
seeing his puny, unprofitable size
had slugged him after with a rifle butt

And he had crawled
to the country roadside
where I came upon him, his fur dust-covered.

Hard to believe
a fox is ever dead, that he isn't
just lying there pretending with his eyes shut.

His fame's against
him; one suspects him of anything,
even when there's blood oozing from the shut eyes.

His evident
self-enjoyment is against him also:
no creature so wild and gleeful can ever be done for.

But this fox was;
there's no place in the world any more
for free and gallant predators like him.

Eagle, lion,
fox and falcon: their freedom is their death.
Man, animal tamed and tainted, wishes to forget.

He prefers bears
in cages: delights to see them pace
back and forth, swatting their bars despondently.

Yet hates himself,
knowing he's somehow contemptible:
with knives and libraries the dirtiest predator of all.

Ghost of small fox,
hear me, if you're hovering close
and watching this slow red trickle of your blood:

Man sets even
more terrible traps for his own kind.
Be at peace; your gnawed leg will be well-revenged.

THE PHYLACTERY BOX

Commandant
of one of the exterminating *gruppen*
operating on the Eastern Front
he gassed
nearly a quarter-million Jews

Once only
on an impulse
he spared a young Jewess
who reminded him
of someone he knew
back home in Hamburg

In 1976
one of the grey-haired
murderers
still among us
he piously touches the memory
of that impulse
like my father
the phylactery box on his forehead
and looks out at the world
with clear blue honest eyes
a friendly light
shining always in them

THE FINAL SOLUTION

It's been all cleared away, not a trace:
laughter keeps the ghosts in the cold ovens
and who can hear the whimpering of small children
or of beaten men and women, the hovering echoes,
when the nickelodeons play all day the latest Berliner
love ballads, not too loudly, just right?
Taste the blood in the perfect Rhenish wine
or smell the odour of fear when such lovely
well-scented Frauleins are fiddling with the knobs
and smiling at the open-faced soldier in the corner?

History was having one of its fits — so what?
What does one do with a mad dog? One shoots it
finally and returns armless and bemedalled
to wife and children or goes to a Chaplin film
where in the accommodating dark the girlfriend
unzips your fly to warm her hands on your scrotum.
Heroes and villains, goodies and baddies, what
will you have to drink with your goulash? In art museums
together they're shown the mad beast wagging its tail
at a double-hooked nose that dissolves into ash

And appraised by gentlemen with clean fingernails
who admire a well-executed composition or pointed to
in hushed tones so that nothing of the novel *frisson*
be lost. Europe blew out its brains
for that *frisson*: gone forever are the poets and actors
the audacious comics that made Vienna and Warsaw
hold their sides with laughter. Gone, gone forever.
They will never return, these wild extravagant souls:
mediocrity stopped up their witty mouths,
envy salted the ground with their own sweet blood

Sealed up their light in the lightless halls of death.
Alas, the world cannot endure too much poetry:

a single cracked syllable — with a cognac — suffices.
I have seen the children of *reingemacht* Europe, their
queer incurious dead eyes and handsome blank faces,
leather straps and long matted hair their sole madness.
They have no need of wit or extravagance, they have
their knapsacks, their colourful all-purpose knapsacks.
The nickelodeon grinds on like fate, six fatties play cards:
the day is too ordinary for ghosts or griefs

EINE KLEINE NACHTMUSIK

I was nowhere near
the syphilitic whore called Europe
smelling of charnel houses and museums

And was not there
when you ripped open the bellies
of pregnant women

Nor when you laughed uproariously
at the spectres
clawing one another for offal

I was not there when you made skeletons
dance for you
and grief-crazed Jewesses to sing

If you're dead
you're beyond my curses and contempt
inviolable as a jackal's calcified turd

But alive and still insurable,
you're probably in Obersalzburg
letting Mozart ravish your souls

Or in Budapest, Vilna, Cologne
buying sausages, perhaps
Xmas toys for your grandchildren

Why not? Since power's the world's standard
it's your victims, not you,
who feel besmirched and guilty

Ah, *meine herren*, we live in a time
when atrocity's the norm
and survival the sole merit

In 1980 everyone lives
with some gas in his lungs.
No one will die of it

MIDSUMMER'S DREAM IN THE VIENNA STADPARK

Auschwitz, as we know, is on the moon
And Belsen on Mars or Venus.
How can I not believe it?
The waltz strains are so entrancing

Anne Frank is alive and well
And so's her sister Margot;
In fact they're right here in the park
Seated beside the gentleman in the third row.

How handsome the two sisters look
— Anne's eyes, as always, are radiant;
They are drinking in the music
And can scarcely keep their feet from dancing.

And they praise the statue of Johann Strauss,
A single curve of pure delight;
Time sleeps on his violin
And he smiles at them all through the night.

Someone has gone to find their father;
He should be here any minute now.
Ah, happy man, run fast, faster,
Do not stop to wipe your brow.

For all in the park recognize Anne
And stand up as one to applaud her
Because though doomed herself she wept
When she saw gypsy children led to the gas chamber.

FOR ANNE FRANK

Now many will live by your name

Because you are only a child
without medals and crucifixes,
a promise of goodness and talent
broken in half by the world's brutal hand

A tender lyric an equivocal destiny
forbade to grow into fertile splendour,
and the anguish of unfulfilment
in the inconsolable tears of each of us

Anne, the abandoned of God
who yet sought and found Him
hiding behind your great terror:
who cloaked Him with your faith and love

A legend on your smiling lips
you move gently into the future
that greets you with the light
from your own sombre eyes and laughter.

DEPARTED

I walk the streets
of Amsterdam
            looking
everywhere for the faces
Rembrandt painted

The visages of burghers
unruffed and unruffled
(though a suspicion
in the clear light eyes
            the world's not always
ordered for the best)
arise to confront me

Unchanged
as the weather-stained gables
in their chartered banks
in their sleek pleasure boats

But where
are gone the grizzled ecstatic
faces
        of the vehement crazy men
who dreamed and prayed?

THE LATEST WRINKLE

Last night at the Neptune
sipping my thick coffee and cognac
I heard the woman exclaim
and believe me everyone
there was such
an unmistakable depth of feeling
in her voice, such
a real unaffected sincerity,
her words burnt themselves into my mind:

"Some of my best friends, Mr. Cohen,
are Jewish survivors from Majdanek
and Auschwitz!"

THE ELECTION

My star-crossed brothers,
envy
is so perverse
in its manifestations,
so abominates
all distinctions
between man and man,
the distressed Christians dream
of burning you
all over again
in improved ovens
because *you* were elected
and not *they*
for the martyrdom
of the Holocaust

DAS WAHRE ICH

She tells me she was a Nazi; her father also.
Her brother lies buried under the defeat
    and rubble of Stalingrad.
She tells me this, her mortal enemy, a Jew.

We are twenty years removed from war.
She urges on me candied biscuits and tea,
and her face is touched by a brief happiness
when I praise her for them and for the mobiles
    she has herself fashioned
in the comfortless burdensome evenings.

Her face is sad and thin as those mobiles
moving round and round in the small wind
my voice makes when I thank her
and she bows her frail proud head into her hands.

The terrible stillness holds us both
and stops our breath
while I wonder, a thrill stabbing into my mind:
    "At this moment, does she see my crumpled form
    against the wall,
blood on my still compassionate eyes and mouth?"

FOR 7515-03296

Your eyes are dark and tragic as history
as you stare at the postcard village in the distance;
you are a distinguished graduate from Auschwitz
and mankind's incurable viciousness,
and your slender arm with its tattooed figures
boldly displays your credentials to the world

Each time, my dear, I see your naked loveliness
on this deserted beach my heart is torn apart
by love and loathing, gratitude and disgust,
by reverence and rage until my frantic mind
scurries like that insect between the hot stones
and I grow deaf to all but the waves' savage gulps

And though I know that all the innocent dead
find their resurrection in us and every loving pair;
imaging the dateless horror of the death camp;
the lexicon of human villainy made plain,
I curse without ceasing into the sweet empty air
and feel my loathing for mankind grow as vast as the sea

TO THE VICTIMS OF THE HOLOCAUST

Your terrible deaths are forgotten;
no one speaks of them anymore.

The novelty of tattooed forearms
wore off quickly; people now say
your deaths are pure invention, a spoof.

More corrosive of human pride
than Copernicus or Darwin, your martyrdoms
must lie entombed in silence.

The devil himself is absolved, polyhistors
naming him the only fascist in Europe
ignorant you were changed into soap and smoke.

That's how the wind blows. Tomorrow
some *goy* will observe you never existed
and the Holocaust your just deserts
for starting wars and revolutions.

I live among the blind, the deaf, and the dumb.
I live among amnesiacs.

My murdered kin
let me be your parched and swollen tongue
uttering the maledictions
bullets and gas silenced on your lips.

Fill, fill my ears with your direst curses.
I shall tongue them, unappeasable shades,
till the sun turns black in the sky.

TO THE JEWISH DISSENTERS

Always the same story:
the Jew against the world

Always the same red-faced goons
drunk with power
and shouting insults

And always the same fate
befalling the gentile nation
menacing him:

Obloquy
and, very mercifully,
swift oblivion

O Babylon, O Persia, O Rome
where are your trophies . . .
where are your triumphs and ambassadors. . . .

PARQUE DE MONTJUICH

I

In European cemeteries my brothers lie
neither ignored nor neglected; they cause
not even a tremor of shame or embarrassment
but if sometimes thought of, thought of then
as something heteroclite — even intriguing —
like a freakish trinket whose origin has been forgotten

How clean-smelling, how green and fertile
this park, once a Jewish cemetery
where they hauled in the broken bones from the nearby
      ghetto;
One wonders, standing beside these shrubs, these trees,
did the grass come up cleaner, darker
for marrow and flesh being occasionally toasted

Yet, look! Beyond the tourist museums Columbus,
in his molten arms the blood of Marranos,
proudly turns his back on the cathedrals and whores;
standing high above the city on his astrolabe
he points his raised finger to the New World
beyond these foul streets, the polluted stinking harbours

II

Prickly as the Jews whose dust they cover
these grotesque misshapen cacti
climb the hot and dusty mountainsides

110

They cluster in green squalid ghettos
contorting like Hebrew letters some hand dispersed
upon this arid, inhospitable ground

Between them, catching at once mind and eye
the vivid perennial blood-drops of geraniums
that thrive, their stems cut again and again

While towering above red flowers, cacti and rock
brood the dark rabbinical cypresses
giving coolth and dignity to their anguished flock

     III

I sit on the weatherbeaten bench. Before me
the busy harbour; yet all that I can see
are the round-roofed steel sheds and cranes
between stone pillars making a perfect
focus for my dazzled eyes. They select
the sheer lines rising grey and plain
though tilting all ways starkly
as if in abstract collusion with the cacti
my gaze takes in on either side
each time I turn my marvelling head

Yet here where each bloom is green or red
where botanists might feel wholly glad
to touch exotic shrubs, flowers, towering palmtrees
I see clearly framed between those pillars now
the black phylactery box on my father's brow
blotting out nature's joyful variety;

smell below these neatly parterred stones
the detritus of long-forgotten flesh and bones
and hear all morning no other sound
but Rachel's voice rising from the ground

Barcelona,
August 6, 1975

MONTJUICH: *The old Montes Judaicus, i.e., "Jewish Mountain." It was here that the Jews of Barcelona had their burial ground. Now it is an elegantly laid-out park overlooking the harbour and the old part of the city.*

RHINE BOAT TRIP

The castles on the Rhine
are all haunted
by the ghosts of Jewish mothers
looking for their ghostly children

And the clusters of grapes
in the sloping vineyards
are myriads of blinded eyes
staring at the blind sun

The tireless Lorelei
can never comb from her hair
the crimson beards
of murdered rabbis

However sweetly she sings
one hears only
the low wailing of cattle-cars
moving slowly across the land

THE SHADOW

I am a shadow. Everywhere, in the house
where I slip from my wife's embrace
as if her daily kiss turns me
inexplicably into vapour or a black cloud,
at the university where I teach teenagers
how to hide their emptiness and grow richer
than corn factors during a famine; even
my youngest son whom I love best
for he's my own childhood raised from
a cemetery of lies and guilts
cannot keep the awful metamorphosis
from happening or my uncontrollable
spastic feet from the trap-door that sends me
swinging into space over the loneliest wolves

I release my shadow like a switchblade
or the cavernous grin of a ghost
as it spreads across the polished banister
in failing traces that punctuate and pass,
even here in this well-lighted
Viennese *hofbrau* bursting with bodies
in clotted happy families of three or four
poised to reactivate bowel movements
through *brauten* and *schweinerfleisch*, to grease
with assorted dainties the secretions
of gland and skinpore; or playing cards
and drinking beer making a racket to awaken
Stahrenberg or that runt Dolfuss from the dead

I sit at my table, *nein*, excuse me,
lie flat against the wall and manipulate
my filled glass like an aging acrobat
taking care not to spill a single drop
on their mothballed Nazi uniforms

or the undistinguished guttural faces
of the wives blanched by too much Catholic
piety — or is it pastry? Who wants to be
censorious at a moment like this, a moralist
when all are good-naturedly enjoying
the warm summery evening without a care,
stuffing their grudges against the world
a whole lifetime of self-hatred and resentment
into the tumblers they clink with friends
or in happy encircling arc with their neighbours?

Take me off the wall I shout from the wall,
don't leave me stretched out like some African skin
in a museum after the lights are extinguished
or like the silent spear in a corner absurd
and powerless menacing the ceiling;
teach me your indifference to great events
your boisterous pink-faced affability as you slam
down your cards on the table as if they were fists
on an old Jew's skull, let me revel
in your ordinariness, in your guiltless murders
and the inescapable doom of your mediocrity
as you waltz down the Taborstrasse
with the Strausses, *vater* and *sohn*, directing
the orchestra with the baton of a clipped moustache

Teach me, O wretched modern clods
with lies and carnage in your genitalia,
how to love you, how to love every creature
on whom my shadow falls, humbled by the appalling
necessity that placed you here so that galaxies
may be explored and a divine few finally
defile through a ravine suspended only
by sunlight and music. Let me hug

you all to my breast, your mouths slavering
with goodwill and sincerity, my own no less
white and damp, I shout, but who hears my cries?
No one, no one. A tall man dressed for a fashionable
funeral at the Opera House rises invisibly
from one of the tables and gliding towards the door
scrapes off my shadow with his blue fingernails:
at dawn I grope my way to my child's hand

JEWISH MAIN STREET

And first, the lamp-posts whose burning match-heads
Scatter the bog fires on the wet streets;
Then the lights from autos and store windows
That flake cool and frothy in the mist
Like a beaten colloid.
In this ghetto's estuary
Women with offspring appraise
The solemn hypocrisies of fish
That gorp on trays of blue tin . . .
They enter the shops
And haggle for a dead cow's rump.

Old Jews with memories of pogroms
Shuffle across menacing doorways;
They go fearfully, quietly;
They do not wish to disturb
The knapsack of their sorrows.

O here each anonymous Jew
Clutches his ration book
For the minimum items of survival
Which honoured today — who knows? —
Tomorrow some angry potentate
Shall declare null and void.

POST-CREMATORIA

Grey-haired, soft-spoken, and her blue eye bright,
No, she's not your graceless anti-Semite;
For while decrying them does she not use
That nice word *Israelites* instead of *Jews?*

COMRADE TROTSKY

So you wanted the vodka-besotted *moujiks*
to stop calling you Ikey or Itzig
and embrace you as one of their own

And to prove to them you deserved their love
you gave commands to incarcerate and kill
and wore your cavalry boots like a cossack

You even raved about freedom and brotherhood.
Naar! Such prophecies are not for *moujiks*:
they don't know how to apprehend them

In their intolerable perplexity
they float them on rivers and oceans of blood
or use them to paper their Gulags

You were sadly mistaken, Bronstein:
goyim can only be comrades to death.
For your pains you got an icepick in your skull

HELLS

Jean-Paul, you're wrong: hell's not other people
though wrought by them; and of course for others,
not for themselves. Man, a sick animal,
his disappointments armed with an excuse
— a differing opinion, size of ears —
can mutilate a woman's lovely breast
or split in two a venerable skull.

I read some blacks opened six tourists' throats
and painted the beach pebbles with their gore.
Nowadays it could turn out my neighbour
who attends to his roses every night
and lends me his tools to repair my shed
one leaden hour will be my torturer
to hang me by my thumbs till I am dead.

Sectarians can dream of a green place
that purged through suffering men might enter;
of Hell as a providential staircase
that winds its crooked way up to heaven;
if it's blessedness that the sinner craves
redemption is nigh, and so is God's grace:
one day the trumpets blow and he is saved.

But we've seen the fatal arithmetic
of the Selection make all virtues vain:
the shade is patterned to the lamp and room
though the skin once encased a selfless man,
the soap smells no sweeter for his fragrance.
In our modern hells, accident and chance
save; not goodness, not love or providence.
Today, one guards not one's soul but a spoon.

YOU NEVER CAN TELL

You fool, keep quiet
about the Holocaust!

There are Christians
who haven't heard
and it might give them
ideas.

ANARCH

My uneasiness before trees. Nothing
cures me of it or ever will. I'm one
my humanity dooms to gaze at their tall
composed shapes with longing; praying
for bright-wing'd insects to stitch me

By their sallies, their senseless thrusts
into the green palmate leaves I see filtering
the viscous sunshine into a rose decanter
each opened bud this tranquil morning
offers the surrounding thoughtless air

My head's too stuffed with griefs
contemporary and classical to know
beneficence today as any grey trunk proud
of its leafy medallions and fluttering them
like a Soviet commander for all to see

A decaying bug-eyed humanist, I rot
into this murderous century, smiling
tolerantly in all directions, my
blue and gentle eyes beseeching forgiveness
for the compost odours rising like a tide

But sometimes I turn my eyeballs around
to see my skull's interior, become
a mad neurologist and probe with poised lens
the mechanism of brainfold and nerve
that ticks towards the bright disaster

That must one day blot out the heavens,
the agony of innocents caught like a lynx
in the steel trap of human malice
or harpooned like those other Jews,
the harried whales of the prosperous sea.

Niagara-on-the-Lake
August 17, 1980

ON THE SUDDEN DEATH OF A RELATIVE

So you up and died.
Just like that!
And no human, no demented ape
for power or money
or a tinsel glory
did you in
but let you live out
your allotted span.

Here in Niagara-on-the-Lake
encircled by orchards,
vineyards and bland foreheads
I rejoice and imagine you
grey-haired and handsome
without crushed bones
or twisted limb.

In these brutal times
Rilke would have approved
your easy death, as I do
who marvel at your luck
and send you love

THE HAEMORRHAGE

I am here. The year is haemorrhaging badly.
Nothing can stanch the flow. Go see for yourself
the bloody kerchiefs accumulating in my backyard.
Countless: more flung down every minute
in a comedy of despair. The wind turns up its blast.

Names I give to the reddest leaves dropping
past my window: Hitler, Stalin, Mussolini.
Brilliantly they fared and flared for a season;
now they will lie in a heap, one on top of another,
turning to muck in the surrounding ordinary grass.

Dynasties, civilizations flutter past me
in a rain of blood: those that were, those yet to be.
Europe bleeding to death with its murdered Jews. Finis.
The infected brown leaf crimson at the edges has begun to
    fall.
I listen for the noiseless splash in the immense blood-pool
    below.

ADAM

I wish we could go back
to the beginning

When there were no hospitals
and no churches dispensing
the analgesics of religion,
not even the famous eye-tingling one
in Milan, the *Duomo*;
no typewriters furiously clicking out
for the jocoseness of cherubs and angels
our latest humiliation and impotency;
when there were no circus freaks
Fellini freaks, speedfreaks, Jesusfreaks
no Seventh Day Adventists, Scientologists
apocalyptics, epileptics, eupeptics, and sceptics
and no bloated greedyguts
stuffing their diseased bladders
with paper money and gold,
no courtesans lining their perfumed orifices
with expensive many-hued crystals
amassed at Cusy's

Before the human larynx acquired
its tinge of querulous dissatisfaction
and mind became a forever open wound
of militant self-serving cynicism and doubt

Before Caesar crossed the Rubicon
because there was no Rubicon to cross
and no Alexander the Dardanelles
because there was no Dardanelles
and no Alexander handsome and mad;
no Darius, no Sarpedon, no Xerxes
no Pharaohs, no Baals, no Astarte
no Chinese dynasties or ideograms

nurturing in their mysterious script
Maoism and the Long March

There's only God and myself
in the cool first evening in Eden
discussing his fantastic creation,
the moon and the stars,
and the enveloping stillness.
About the woman
he has in mind for me
we talk softly and for a long time
and very, very carefully.

RABBI SIMEON COMFORTS HIS FLOCK

My abused people
you go staggering under blow after blow:
Germany, Russia, Poland.
Always there's an Egypt to flee.

Children of sorrow and light,
you are God's seed
and His sower's hand
scatters you over the earth.

Other's rest cozy and proud in empire
until your bleeding feet
traversing their soil in flight
erase them from His sight forever.

JUDEA ETERNA

Where are the Roman legions, where is Titus
Against whose mouldering arch the passing Jew pisses?

PAUL SEXTUS

That fine ascetic, exemplar
of Christian alertness
and solicitude,
is distressed by embattled Israel
raiding remote guerrilla camps

Yet nearly six million Jews
went up in smoke
in full view of the Vatican
without a single peep from any pope
or cardinal

Mgr. Frascati assures me
it was the fumes climbing
their oversensitive nostrils
that tickled their throats
and made them choke

ON THE DEATH OF POPE PAUL VI

An animal dies
and rots back into the earth

Vanquished crustaceans
are washed up by the tide

A swordfish is hooked
and turned into feces and gas

But a pope greets Monsignor Death
with a mitre on his head

Red slippers on his feet

And formaldehyde in his veins

SIGHTSEEING

When the distinguished Israeli
visitor
was asked by the guide
what he most wanted
to see
during his stay
in the Federal Republic
he replied
after only a moment's
delay:

"German cemeteries."

HERZL

Vain and multivalent as all Jews have been
— half-ass playwright, fop, boulevardier
and Viennese decadent with death in your nostrils —
your poet's vision powered a flight of bullets

Alternately racked by melancholia and fervour
and taking all of Europe for your stage
you peopled it with kings, intriguers, sultans, popes,
yourself least aware where truth began, feigning stopped

Self-hypnotized as maddened poets anywhere,
charismatic fraud and lovable charlatan,
you dared will fantasy into stubborn political fact
undaunted that all dreams birth the discrepant act

And just when old kingdoms, old philosophies
were dissolving into *fin-de-siècle* crimson mist
and Hegel's conquering World Spirit hovered
on ominous wing over the gutters of Vienna

Your magic raised a nation out of bloodsoaked ruts:
from crowded halls rose the dust whom cossacks
and renowned statesmen and priests had thwacked
into the slums of Europe's festering capitals

Who but yourself, Herzl, ever turned stagecraft
into superb statecraft? Lord Byron, true poet,
tried and failed. D'Annunzio. You only would get
vision and energy into one brilliant, flawless act

NEXT YEAR, IN JERUSALEM

There is evil
and men are given over wholly
to pride,
pitiless in their reach
for power and glory

Yet Anatoli Shcharansky
didn't betray his comrades
and Ginzburg
ill and defenceless
defied the Soviet empire

Lonely opposing martyrs,
in the desolation of their cities
the besotted slavemasters
will recall your words,
the flames carrying on their backs
the furious contempt of Isaiah
shrivelling their insolence
into black cinders

I kiss your hands;
across steppes and barbed wire
send you my heartfelt greetings

Next year, in Jerusalem!

JEW

Someone
who feels himself to be
a stranger
            everywhere

Even in Israel

ISRAELIS

It is themselves they trust and no one else;
Their fighter planes that screech across the sky,
Real, visible as the glorious sun;
Riflesmoke, gunshine, and rumble of tanks.

Man is a fanged wolf, without compassion
Or ruth: Assyrians, Medes, Greeks, Romans,
And devout pagans in Spain and Russia
— Allah's children, most merciful of all.

Where is the Almighty if murder thrives?
He's dead as mutton and they buried him
Decades ago, covered him with their own
Limp bodies in Belsen and Babi Yar.

Let the strong compose hymns and canticles,
Live with the Lord's radiance in their hard skulls
Or make known his great benevolences;
Stare at the heavens and feel glorified

Or humbled and awestruck buckle their knees:
They are done with him now and forever.
Without a whimper from him they returned,
A sign like an open hand in the sky.

The pillar of fire: their flesh made it;
It burned briefly and died — you all know where.
Now in their own blood they temper the steel,
God being dead and their enemies not.

THE NEW SENSIBILITY

Never mind
beating out your exile, Ez:
that's literary hogwash,
vintage quaintsville

A more efficacious
epigram
for stopping the mouths
of tormentors
is a bullet in the head:
it opens a hole
and closes the matter forever

Tamed bears
toothless tigers
caged lions
defenceless ghetto Jews
(Polacks to Nazis in Warsaw circa 1941:
nab them, nab them, they're Jews!)
and poets
who dish out the familiar idealistic crap
always make the murderous crowd
slobber
preparatory to prodding them with sticks
and pouring gasoline on their cadavers

The up-to-date poet
besides labouring at his craft
should be a dead shot

Do you hear me, Old Man?
a dead shot
sending the bullet

winging like a finished stanza
straight between the eyes

That's the new poetry
minted June 1967
in Tel Aviv and Sinai

I thought
I should let you know

POET AT SINAI

Corpses fingering blood-stained triggers
seem to the poet a grim charade
who sees the silent, bloated figures
lying like balloons in a parade.

Crushed tanks: their oil bleeding into sand
that a wild molecular frenzy
into dark hieroglyphs changes; and
outlines of a desolate beauty.

Arms raised to salute the victory
by sightless soldiers that have no breath.
Let the victors rejoice; he only
tells them of the cardboard smell of death

HA-NAGID'S ADMONITION TO JEWISH
SCHOLARS

Waste no time unriddling the anti-Semite;
That won't save you when you have to fight or run.
Learn well in the hours still given to you
How to slash with a knife, how to fire a gun.

THE BEST PROOF

Love your neighbour
and labour daily
    at proving
how much you love him

By making yourself
so powerful
    nothing can ever
tempt him to injure you

RECIPE FOR A LONG AND HAPPY LIFE

Give all your nights
to the study of Talmud

By day practice
shooting from the hip

MEMO TO MY SONS

Remember, my sons,
   man is an animal
who has a soul:
different from giant reptiles
hawks
and repulsive monsters
                 in forest
and sea
he wants to kill
with a good conscience

Speak softly
   to this queer beast;
soothe him, soothe him

SHALOM SHALOM

Reflect well on this, my sons:
that when you look and speak like a god,
your face handsome for the sun
your eyes bright with health and gladness
    and the ventricles of your heart
dilating with goodwill for all mankind
for everything astir with life and joy
what the virtuous egalitarian
wants more than anything else to do
    just then
is to smash your face in!

FOR MY SONS, MAX AND DAVID

The wandering Jew: the suffering Jew
The despoiled Jew: the beaten Jew
The Jew to burn: the Jew to gas
The Jew to humiliate
The cultured Jew: the sensitized exile
    gentiles with literary ambitions aspire to be
The alienated Jew cultivating his alienation
    like a rare flower: no gentile garden is complete
    without one of these bleeding hibiscus
The Jew who sends Christian and Moslem theologians
    back to their seminaries and mosques for new arguments
    on the nature of the Divine Mercy
The Jew, old and sagacious, whom all speak well of:
    when not lusting for his passionate, dark-eyed daughters
The Jew whose helplessness stirs the heart and conscience
    of the Christian like the beggars outside his churches
The Jew who can be justifiably murdered because he is rich
The Jew who can be justifiably murdered because he is poor
The Jew whose plight engenders profound self-searchings
    in certain philosophical gentlemen who cherish him
    to the degree he inspires their shattering aperçus
    into the quality of modern civilization, their noble
    and eloquent thoughts on scapegoatism and unmerited
        agony
The Jew who agitates the educated gentile, making him pace
    back and forth in his spacious well-aired library
The Jew who fills the authentic Christian with loathing for
        himself
    and his fellow Christians
The Jew no one can live with: he has seen too many
        conquerers
    come and vanish, the destruction of too many empires
The Jew in whose eyes can be read the doom of nations
    even when he averts them in compassion and disgust

The Jew every Christian hates, having shattered his
       self-esteem
   and planted the seeds of doubt in his soul
The Jew everyone seeks to destroy, having instilled
       self-division
   in the heathen

Be none of these, my sons
My sons, be none of these
Be gunners in the Israeli Air Force

AFTER AUSCHWITZ

My son,
don't be a waffling poet;
let each word you write
be direct and honest
like the crack of a gun

Believe an aging poet
of the twentieth century:
neither the Old Testament
nor the New
or the sayings of the Koran
or the Three Baskets of Wisdom
or the Dhammapada
will ever modify or restrain
the beastliness of men

Lampshades
were made from the skins
of a people
preaching the gospel of love;
the ovens of Auschwitz and Belsen
are open testimony
to their folly

Despite memorial plaques
of horror and contrition
repentance, my son,
is short-lived

An automatic rifle
endures
a lifetime

TO MAOISTS

From my heart I rooted out Jehovah;
I spurned Moses and his Tables of Law
And tore up my father's phylacteries.
I did not turn from dragons to live with fleas.

NIGHTMARE IN THE ANNEX

My friend, a post-Holocaust half-Jew, lives
on the same street as I, oceans
and black volcanic mountain ranges apart.
   We sometimes meet when sorrow makes a space
or it might be it's rage will flutter
out of his mouth, a broken-winged raven
to light a circle of fire to keep me inside:
but good moments come soon like cooling rains.

A fractured demi-Jew, his woe is doubled:
well-scrubbed and providentially handsome
he passes for a WASP in darkest Toronto until
   he speaks about Jews and starts to rave.
Then his fine-cut features turn deep pink,
the voice becoming guttural, not his own.
That's when something strange comes over me,
and malice making its pitch, I call him *Pinchas.*

Though I love him like a younger brother
genetics too will claim its sad martyrs,
squads of cripples whose favourite mainstays are
   hymns that comfort, words of song and poetry
unheard above the world's loud churn of hate.
My compassion's a poor thing, streaked
with insult, knowing the hellfire Europe loosed
on those Jews who praised life till life was gone.

A small restless animal tied to his trunk,
his right arm's seeming autonomy
puts a squint into his frank grey eyes
   as though the limb had a mind of its own
wanting to put distance between his father's beard
and himself. Or is it fear the wilful fingers
will snatch up onion slices and herring,
the wife cool and impeccably English at his side?

SANCTA SIMPLICITAS

Write me a poem, said Reb Magid,
simple and uncomplicated
as a little spaniel;
show me —
a humble, hungering man —
God's careful mercy
in the fell
and the four warm paws
placed on His field of glory.

And staring at the pupils
of his guiltless eyes
I could see
they were of the same
elemental order
as a bird,
as bread or a tree,
and it was clear
that I and the angels knew
what the good man meant.

But a breath later, catching
behind his curved
complacent back
my face's pale reflection
in the windowpane,
I became confused
and to his elation
bitterly silent.

SUNFLOWERS

How majestic they were
a bare month ago, tall-erect;
now bare but for petals
that reach out like begging hands.

Blind Oedipus and his companion,
they lean against the air
and mock the betraying sun.

The morning glory's faded beauty
is no comfort, nor the white ash of my cigar.
I know what I know. Everything flows;
living, dies: the intruding dog in my garden,
the butterflies cavorting
over the plundered mounds. The white disaster
is on the way
and will not be stopped.

I think of the young Marx,
heaven-storming Promethean, making
kings and capitalists quake
with his *Grundrisse*, his black smouldering eyes
— praising unalienated man, Superman!

"I sowed dragons' teeth and reaped pygmies."

No, my red Messiah, tempestuous Jew.
Your sunflower beauty still flourishes;
astonishes, still rouses man-enslaved man,
poet and mad philosopher
at noonday and in the stillest hour of the night.

THE ANNUNCIATION

What angels will we meet on the way to the post office?
What kisses will the leaves rain down on your neck?
Your footsteps leave no shadows on the ground
for the morning sun makes a bale of them
which he tosses over the first white fence that we pass

The announcing angel robes himself in ordinary dress.
What name does he whisper in your perfumed
and delicate ear? Judith? Deborah? Eve?
When you incline your fragrant head to listen,
the storewindows blaze and shine and the village street

Robed in its summer foliage resounds like a West Point
salute with the sound of champagne bottles uncorked;
all the birds in the street take the happy noise
for cues and suddenly whole orchestras of them
and the singing choirs of girls and boys

Make such a jubilation, it frightens off
all evils and sorrows forever; your burgeoning form
parts the air before us like a sorcerer's wand
and the angel in ordinary dress extricates a wing
and blesses its bounty with his own bright feathers

Niagara-on-the-Lake
June 4, 1980

152

FOR ELSE LASKER-SCHULER

They came: the uncircumcised Jews from Alexandria,
bringing self-contempt and parchment
to the thinnest rivulets of Germany, energizing
the blond hordes with an ancient sickness

Soon crosses studded the land, marking
the progress of the disease from field to field;
vapour from the mouths of decrepit monks
enveloped the churchspires with the loud peal of bells

Like a trichinosis or forest fire
it must burn itself out, leaving behind
the smell of cellars and charred flesh;
fears be blown about like dandelion seeds

Only after many hatreds, superstitions,
the pawnshops overflowing with cardinals' rings,
prophecies will be stamped *korrekt*
and issued the necessary passports

Whoever is overtaken by one of them
becomes a master without slave or lackey
and invincible through grief and inner freedom
greets the morning sun with laughter

FATHER AND DAUGHTER

My daughter is sleeping;
when she isn't sleeping she catches
beauty on the wing
and pins it to one of her walls
as a picture of a rose or seascape,
a Matisse or an illuminated painting
her own hands have made;
she has beauty flowering
out of discarded winebottles

Or trailing its serrated leaves
down the sides of cupboards.
I believe she has even learned how to make
the sunshine lie down on her carpets
in mandated patterns and designs;
certainly tables with jars are altars
and wherever my eyes fall
they alight on something that gives pleasure
and reminds one of eternity

A cynical aging Jew
who knows much about men's
incurable viciousness and brutality,
their sodden penchant for evil,
I marvel at a serenity
that has endured wars and holocausts,
at a faith that finds goodness
the heart and core of this universe
— at this curious product of my own loins!

Every five years or so
I visit my daughter now lovely woman
and delighting guitarist;
I grow more savage with the affrighting years,
my poems more bitter and scornful

so that they are stones I scatter
in fusillades of mockery and hate:
my daughter each time I see her
has another illuminated rose on the wall.

San Francisco
July 9, 1978

SENILE, MY SISTER SINGS

Senile, my sister sings. She sings
the same snatch of song over and over
in a quivering voice, her lips trembling
when she tries for the high notes. Her white
hair close-cropped like a prisoner's
and her unobstructed tongue lolling
over her furrowed lip while her dentures
grin at us through a glass of water,
my sister is some kind of vocal chicken,
especially when her small raisin eyes dart
from visitor to visitor as though about
to pluck worms out of their garments.
My heart breaks remembering her beauty
and wit, the full mouth with a tale in it
she finally exploded in our ears.
Is this my sister so frail and emaciated,
whose valour and go were family legends,
her smiles so dazzling they made the roaches
leisurely roaming the walls of our kitchen
scurry behind the torn wallpaper
to hide there till the incandescence had passed?
Sing, my dear sister, sing
though your trembling lips break my heart
and I turn away from you to sob
and let the tears course down my cheeks,
my grief held back by pride and even a kind
of exultance. You do not moan or whimper,
you do not grovel before the Holy Butcher
and beg Him to spare you days; or rock
silently like the other white-haired biddies
waiting to be plucked from their stoops. No,
though His emissary ominously flaps his wings
to enfold you in their darkness, you sing.
Your high-pitched notes must rile him

more than rage or defiance. You sing him
no welcome, and if your voice trembles
it's not fear or resignation he hears
but the cracked voice of the *élan vital*
whose loudest chorister you are, abashing Death
and making him skulk in his own shadow.

BOSCHKA LAYTON: 1921—1984

Because each act of creation is a miracle
that happens again and again
until it becomes familiar as an autumn leaf
or a ripening appletree in full sail

I shall remember you not as charred bone and ash
to be given to earth's mad alchemy
but as the full-bosomed woman whose lips
mouthed my awed whisper: "We shall make handsome
    children"

Your heart's vital joy apparent in the eyes of friends,
in children's smiles and the smiles of old women,
it is presumptuous to speak now of your crazy defiance
idle to praise the harsh devotions of your life

Ordinary miracles to pry open the eyes of the blind
happen every day. Yet my deep faith holds:
sun, wind, rain, and the dark nights will change
my Boschka's cinders to deathless apples and poems

Santa Rosa
February 17, 1984

158

GRAND FINALE

I've seen grey-haired lyrists come down from the hills;
they think because they howl with eloquence and conviction
the townspeople will forgive their disgraceful sores
and not care how scandalous and odd they look;
how vain their contrite blurtings over booze and women
or the senescent itch for the one true faith.

Not for me sorrowful and inglorious old age
not for me resignation and breastbeating
or reverbing of guilts till one's limbs begin to tremble
and a man's brought to his knees whimpering and ashamed;
not for me if there's a flicker of life still left
and I can laugh at the gods and curse and shake my fist.

Rather than howl and yowl like an ailing cat
on wet or freezing nights, or mumble thin pieties
over a crucifix like some poor forsaken codger
in a rented room, I'll let the darkness come only when I
an angry and unforgiving old man yank the cloth of heaven
and the moon and all the stars come crashing down.

THE WHEEL

By the polluted lake
the terrorized worms keep all their resolutions;
birds fly past my fears,
indifferent to malice or despair
or the book I hold up
to mirror their ecstatic flights.
My stockinged feet might be
stubble rotting back into earth;
the sandals beside them,
dew-wet and modest in the grass
and remaining close to all my contradictions,
those Jeshua wore when he walked on water.
I have divested myself of everything
except some remembered griefs
I roll like spotted dice
which an imaginary hand thrusting
down like water from a spout
scoops up for the return throw.
My friends, it was never my intention
to play games with Time or Fate or Chance
and for certain not with Death
or to scatter foolish words about
in poems and conversation
concerning the weather in my skull.
Who cares how anyone fares
or what devils he exorcises
with a ripe strawberry leaf
or a rusting nail
extracted from an old horseshoe?
If I stretched out on the grass
in mimic sleep or death
the dice would roll over my face,
yet no finger of mine unbend
to arrest the glittering parabolas
brazing dream and reality

or to mute the thunders in my head.
The air would close over me
like water over the demented fish
in the lake,
magnifying the raw welts
which this age
brutal with madmen's fugues
rubbed into my back and shoulders;
the tears swollen and cold
from wild unblinking eyes that stare
at the polluted droplets
erasing into bubble and froth
and once again preparing
the loose folds of my naked flesh
for the next relentless turn of the wheel.

FINAL RECKONING

Me? I feel safest in cemeteries.
Horizontal humans lie peacefully;
no anger or mischief in them, no hate
and deceit. Even if darkness comes
when I find myself standing near a slab
time and fierce squalls have tilted towards me
so that I think of the moles underfoot
tearing the flesh clean off the skeletons
I have no fear or sadness. Why should I?
The dead are surely more fortunate
to be done at last with life's ills and chills,
with the lies needed for mere survival
and the mean compromises each must make
before he can call some small space his own.
Bah! The comedy's not worth a frog's fart;
only priests and rabbis think otherwise,
metaphysicians and crazed bolsheviks.
For myself, I love the tranquil boneyards
both for the evergreen moral they teach
and for the asylum they give against
the violent longings that agitate
the caged animals of Chicago
and Madrid, of Moscow, Belfast and London.
Tombs, I say, are reassuring when men
are swine, smiling wolves with capped teeth,
the cities reeking of scribbling whores
and those who need no bribes to pimp for them.
To these, O Zeus, send plagues! Destroy them all!
Don't leave behind a single specimen
and rid earth of locusts, snakes, and weevils;
let the new seedlings come up tall and green.
Preserve all poets mad and marvellous,
guard them from the fury of envious dust.

162

TWENTIETH-CENTURY GOTHIC

"Ghetto of the elect. A wall, a ditch.
Expect no mercy. In this most Christian
of worlds, the poet is a Jew."

— Marina Tsvetayeva

I wake from a troubled doze and rub my eyes.
The Jew is still whispering his tribal secrets
to the wall, bending his spare frame this way
and that, almost licking the Hebrew words off their page.

The same human carnage flows through his veins as mine,
yet I turn from him in sadness and dismay. He's one
of God's white mice in whose damaged bodies
vaccines are made for the select few, immunizing

Them against a world Divine Justice
made purposively malign. Though his skin's pallor
and burning speechless gaze mark out the fanatic,
the lobby's glare despoils him of mystery and love.

The lighted lobby turns everything commonplace,
diminishes the most barbarous event into a happening
in search of a camera while saints and holy men
beseech the deaf walls for favours and I

God's recording angel loosed in a roaring desert
gape at the blind lens like a once-famous Alpinist
whose name we recall only after a long frozen pause,
a flurry of precipitous promptings.

ETRUSCAN TOMBS

for Dante Gardini

Being so close to death
so many times
why should you be moved, as I am,
by these offenceless ruins?

I ask pardon for my abstracted gaze,
my impatience with your slow speech,
your gentle all-forgiving smile.
I did not spend my best years
in a concentration camp;
no vile humanoid ever
menaced me with gun and whip
or made me slaver for crusts
urine-soiled and stale;
no officered brute made me kneel in shit.

Here beside you in this remote scene
I feel death's cold finger on my skin,
making it twitch like a fly-stung mare's.
Yet these blank eyes sculpted
from grove and hill and rock
before which the centuries have passed unseen
comfort me; inuring me, I say,
to the sorrows our humanity
compels us to inflict on each other.
They teach me to live the free hours with gusto.

Nothing endures forever.
Your pain, my pleasure,
the seconds bear away;

our flesh, Dante, one day
will be such golden dust
as a storyless wind stirs
in an empty vault.

Norchia,
September 18, 1984

WARRIOR POET

King David stood up in his chariot;
The valley was strewn with dead Philistines.
Some draped a stone, some lay as if asleep;
On their broken armour the sun hammered and shone.

The war shouts and cries still rang in his ears;
Before his eyes rider and horse still fell.
Though dazed he could yet praise the Lord of Hosts;
Bravely had his warriors fought that day and well.

But the contorted mouths of the slain asked:
"Why did the Lord will it that we should die?"
And he bade his boy to bring him his harp
And his lips quivering stared blankly at the blank sky.

DAVID AND BATHSHEBA

She gave herself to me and I was her god,
her king: nothing I did or could do
was ever mistaken or wrong. I was her Messiah
among men, tall and well-favoured and strong

As for my near-faultless psalms
in praise of the Lord and men of valour:
over their exulting strains she went simply mad
and would listen to them hour after hour

As God hears me, when I was frightened or sad
I was wise enough in the ways of woman
to keep away from her, aware compassion in women
puts to rout all urgings of desire

Yet before the new moon was in the sky
she was mousing out my frailties, scanning my troubled soul
for lesions and cracks. I took my harp from the wall
and sang to sleep the froward slave and infidel

A WILD PECULIAR JOY

King David, flushed with wine,
   is dancing before the Ark;
the virgins are whispering to each other
and the elders are pursing their lips
   but the king knows the Lord delights
in the sight of a valourous man
dancing in the pride of life.

For the Lord of Israel sometimes
   also reels on drunken feet: see,
in the wayward flight of eagles and moths,
in the thunderstorms and when lightning
   rives the cedars of Lebanon,
O the Lord wheels in blazing footgear
above the hills of Jerusalem.

King David is circling the Ark
   on reeling feet, and he sings:
"Ho, Israelites, hear me! Hear me, everyone!
God himself staggers on drunken feet
   and each night wearing
for raiment the flame of our campfires
He dances in our valleys North and South!"

Black-bearded stalwarts leap up to follow him
   as he stumbles around the Ark;
no one listens, none in the throng is fired
with his wild peculiar joy. So bowing low
   he kisses the Ark thrice
and with a last joyous cry reels singing into his tent
to compose a boisterous hymn in praise of the Lord.